TOP 10 SECRETS

FOR INVESTING SUCCESSFULLY

BARBARA GOTTFRIED HOLLANDER

ROSEN PUBLISHING®

New York

This book is dedicated to Jonathan Gottfried, who invests his time and efforts to help all of us. Thank you.

Published in 2014 by The Rosen Publishing Group, Inc.
29 East 21st Street, New York, NY 10010

First Edition

Library of Congress Cataloging-in-Publication Data

Hollander, Barbara Gottfried.
Top 10 secrets for investing successfully/Barbara Gottfried Hollander.—1st ed.—New York: Rosen, © 2014
            p. cm.—(A student's guide to financial empowerment)
Includes bibliographical references and index.
ISBN: 978-1-4488-9357-7 (Library Binding)
ISBN: 978-1-4488-9371-3 (Paperback)
ISBN: 978-1-4488-9372-0 (6-pack)
1. Finance, personal—Juvenile literature. 2. Investments—Juvenile literature. 3. Saving and investment—Juvenile literature. 4. Finance, personal. 5. Saving and investment. I. Title.
HG4521.H65 2014
332.6'0835

Manufactured in the United States of America

CPSIA Compliance Information: Batch #S13YA: For further information, contact Rosen Publishing, New York, New York, at 1-800-237-9932.

Contents

A high school student works in a student-run silk-screen business that prints T-shirts. Money earned from part-time jobs can be used for investments in your future.

Introduction

It is easy to live in the moment and spend all your money on your wants. Grab lunch with friends! Go shopping for new clothes! Order that concert ticket! Your income from work or an allowance can pay for these things. You may even crave the satisfaction that comes from spending all of your money on today's wants.

Remember that your financial decisions have both short- and long-term consequences. In the short run, you enjoy lunch, new clothes, and the concert. But in the long run, you now have less money for tomorrow's wants. Investing money is about using today's money to earn more money for the future. Can you imagine having even more cash to spend in ten or twenty years? You could afford even more clothes, more restaurant lunches, and more concerts.

Successful investing goes beyond these short-term goals. Think bigger financial goals or purchasable aims. For example, suppose that you earn income from a part-time job. You invest some of the earnings, rather than spend them all. When you graduate, you find a full-time job and invest some of these earnings, too. Soon, you have enough money from your investments to afford a car and a home.

Did you notice that investing is about giving up and gaining? You give up the use of some of your money today in hopes of gaining more money later. You give up some of today's goals, like having new clothes this week, to gain possibly a new car or house in the future. Short-term costs can have big long-term payoffs!

As with all money choices, investing means making decisions and taking risks. Figure out how to invest your money by exploring your options. Investments are not foolproof. You do not automatically earn more money because you invest. Investments are risky because things may not turn out as planned. How do you invest successfully, protect yourself from risks, and increase your chances of reaching your goals? Read on.

Know Your Goals

Successful investing means seeing yourself in the future. Think about where you want to be in five, ten, twenty, and fifty years from now. Talk to your mentors (such as relatives and teachers), and discuss your education, work, and life plans.

- Will you attend college?
- If yes, what kind of college and for how many years?
- How are you going to pay for your schooling?
- Do you want to buy a car or home?
- Would you like to own a business?
- Are you planning to have a family?
- What kind of life do you want when you retire?

Think about your answers to these kinds of lifestyle questions. Envision the kind of life that you want, and be realistic. Next, list the top five financial goals that will help you achieve this life. How can you afford these goals? Invest successfully!

Fascinating Financial Fact

Does money grow on trees? It did when the Aztecs used cacao beans for cash. Just as trees grow bigger with time, so can your earnings from most investments!

Paying for It

Remember that investing today is the key to achieving your long-term goals. How much money will you need? It depends on the costs of your goals and your time frame. For example, suppose your goals include buying a new car and home. According to *Forbes*, the average price of a new car in April 2012 was about $30,000. YCharts, a company that provides analytical tools and marketing trend information to investors, reported that the average price of a new house in August 2012 was about $300,000.

Most people take out loans for big-ticket purchases, such as cars and homes. But you still need to put down a part of the item's cost (the down payment) at the time of purchase. Items that cost more (like a house) require higher down payments. So you need to use more money from your investments to pay for the house than for the car.

Also, beware of rising prices. Consider the cost of college. According to the National Center for Education

Teens usually need help from their parents to buy their first car, unless they have saved most of their earnings from a steady job for several years. Investing helps you achieve your long-term goals such as buying a car. You'll need money for a down payment at the time of purchase and for sales tax, auto insurance, gas, maintenance, and repairs.

Statistics, the average tuition for a four-year public college was $6,381 in 1980. By 2010, it rose to $15,605. Prices usually increase. Your investment money needs to cover the future costs of your goals.

Timing Counts

Next, consider your time frame. It is usually easier to pay for a goal that is farther away. Imagine that your goals include paying for college and buying a home. College is right around the corner, while owning a home is a longer-term

Investing includes using an automated teller machine (ATM) to deposit money in an interest-bearing account.

goal. Suppose that you invest money today. You might have only one to four years' worth of earnings to pay for college. But you would have even more earnings in five to ten years to pay for a house.

To see how timing matters, think of an investment as putting money in the bank. Suppose you deposit $100 in a savings account that earns 10 percent annual interest. Now assume that you will not deposit or withdraw any money from this account. In three years, you have $133.10 in your savings account. You earned $33.10 in interest. But in ten years, you will have $259.37 and $159.37 in interest.

Similar financial goals are usually more easily achieved when they are purchased farther away because you earn more investment money to pay for them. Think back to the financial goal of paying for a house. You are more likely to afford this goal if you have more years for your investments to grow. In other words, buying a house will be financially easier in ten years than in five.

Remember to break up investing into two steps over time. The first step is to save some money. Think about your income and expenses. Income is the money earned from sources such as salaries. Expenses are the costs of goods and services. Do you earn more money than you spend? This additional income is your savings. The second part of investing is to use part or all of your savings to make or increase investments that can help you reach your specific goals.

Determine Your Risk Factor

Successful investing includes determining your risk tolerance. Risk is the chance that things will turn out differently from what you expected. For example, in the early 2000s, many people invested their money in real estate, such as new homes. They hoped that the value of their properties would increase, or gain in value. Then they could sell these properties for more than their purchasing price and earn money.

Think Risk

Suppose that you were a real estate investor in 2006. You bought a building for $300,000 as an investment. You hoped to earn money by selling your property for $350,000. At this time, prices in the U.S. real estate market were rising. But then in 2007, housing prices plummeted. Soon, your property was worth only $250,000. What happened? Your investment actually lost money!

Investments are risky. There is always a chance that you could lose money, rather than earn it.

When the value of an investment such as a house falls below the purchase price, an investor can lose money.

Volatility refers to the risk associated with not knowing how much the value of an investment will change. Reading on, you will see that not all investments are equal. Some are riskier than others. For now, you want to figure out your risk factor because not all investors are created equal, either.

How Risky Are You?

To determine your risk profile, take the test!

(1) Imagine an investment that could double your money. But this investment also carries the same chance that you could lose all of your money. What would you do?

(a) Do not invest
(b) Invest some of your money
(c) Put all of your money into this investment

(2) Congratulations! You are a contestant on *Let's Win Some Money.* Which option would you choose?
(a) $500 in cash
(b) 50 percent chance of winning $1,000
(c) 25 percent chance of winning $2,000

(3) You are stranded on a desert island and have one flare left to signal for help. There is a possibility of a boat in the far distance. What do you do?
(a) Save the flare for another time
(b) Use the flare only when you see the boat
(c) Fire the flare!

If your answers were mostly a's, then you are a conservative investor. You hope to earn money by playing it safe. If

Fascinating
Financial Fact

Did you know that buying a lottery ticket is a risky investment? According to "10 Risky Investments" by Rebecca Fairley Raney, the odds of winning the big prize are "around one in 195 million." Fortunately, most lottery tickets cost only $1!

your answers were mostly b's, then you are a moderate investor. You will take some chances to earn money from your investments. If your answers were mostly c's, then you are the ultimate risk taker. You will gamble it all for the chance of earning big bucks.

Return It

As you may have guessed from the test, riskier investments generally have higher returns. This means that investments with the highest chances of losing money can also earn you

This picture shows a stock market chart. The values of stock investments are constantly changing. Investors earn or lose money when they sell these investments.

the most money. The flip side is true, too. Less risky investments usually have lower returns. These investments have a greater chance that you will earn money (and not lose it). But they also usually earn you less money than riskier investments.

As a teen, you have a *big* advantage in dealing with risk—timing! Suppose that you are an aggressive investor who placed $100 in a very risky investment. You could either double your money quickly or lose 75 percent of it. You take the chance but end up losing $75. Next, you place your $25 in another investment. Over time, it increases to more than $100.

As a young adult, you have many years to ride out your investment returns. For this reason, many financial experts advise young people to make more aggressive investments than older people. Whether you are willing to take more or less risk with your investments depends on your risk level. In other words, did you save the flare or fire it?

Make a Financial Profile

Successful investing is about financially defining yourself. You have already begun by listing your goals and determining your risk tolerance. These items are part of your financial profile, which assesses your potential for reaching your money goals. Your financial profile may not be the same as your friends' or relatives' because it reflects you.

Think Budget

A financial profile also includes your budget information. A budget is a financial plan that lists both income and expenses over a specified amount of time. Income is money that you receive, like wages or an allowance. Expenses consist of money that you spend, such as clothes, food, or concert ticket purchases. If income is greater than expenses, you are saving money. You can use saved money to make or increase investments.

Your budget reveals the amount of money available for regular investments.

You can also use other sources to make initial investments, like monetary birthday or graduation gifts.

For example, suppose that you received a birthday gift of $50 from a grandparent. You decide to invest it. After reading this information, you know that increasing your investment amounts can increase your earnings. You examine your budget and see that you are saving $100 each month. You have some short-term goals, like buying new boots for the winter, and long-term goals, like buying a used car when you graduate college.

Savings and Investments

To address your individual wants, divide your savings between your short-term and long-term goals. You make an initial investment of $50 for long-term goals and decide to contribute $50 each month. After one year, you have contributed $650 toward your long-term goals. Now suppose that your investment is earning a 10 percent annual rate of return. You have also earned about $65 extra just for making this investment!

The savings and investment scenario is based on your budget. List your weekly income and expenses. Do you spend more than you earn? Are your expenses and income equal? In both cases, you will need to decrease your spending or increase your earnings to make regular contributions to your investments. But if your income is greater than your expenses, you are in good shape! You can make regular investment contributions. You just need to figure out how to divide your savings between short-term and long-term goals.

Fascinating Financial Fact

According to Statistic Brain, 25 percent of Americans had no savings as of July 2012. Savings are used for investments to reach long-term goals. Don't miss your opportunity!

[Source: http://www.statisticbrain.com/american-family-financial-statistics]

Make It Happen

Examine your actual financial situation. Do you have money for an initial investment? Explore different sources, such as a birthday gift or checking account. Find out how much your investments require as an initial amount. Can you afford your investment options? If not, look for less expensive ones. Enlist the help of parents or other guardians who may be willing to cosign with you to open investment accounts.

Next, figure out if you can increase your investment on a regular basis, perhaps monthly? Remember that your earnings are a percentage of your investment. You receive more earnings if you invest more money. For example, suppose there is an investment with a 10 percent annual rate of return. Jim invests $100 at the beginning of the year, while David makes an initial investment of $100 and contributes $50 per month for one year.

Who earns more money at the end of one year? David does! He earns almost $44 in interest compared to Jim's $10 interest earnings. Because of both his deposits and earnings, David also has a much bigger investment at the end of the first year. Jim has only $110, while David has $743.99. In general, your investments will grow more quickly if you make regular contributions.

Some situations make it difficult to contribute consistently. For example, you may not save regularly or you may have unexpected expenses, like getting a flat tire. You may also be inconsistent with your money decisions, such as saving $50 one month and only $5 the next month.

But you can still increase your investments when possible, like during the months when you save the most money.

Finally, remember that your financial profile changes as your life changes. Your goals today will be different from your goals in ten years. Today, you are likely a single teenager thinking about graduation, school, and getting a job. Tomorrow, you may be married with children and thinking about paying for a home, a bigger car, and your children's future college bills. Life events and attitudes are part of your financial profile because they affect your goals, risk factor, income, and expenses. As you experience life changes, reassess your financial profile.

Speak the Language

Investing has a language. Understanding financial lingo helps you to choose, track, and earn profits from your investments. For starters, a security describes a kind of investment, such as a stock or bond. Securities have bid prices (prices offered by buyers) and ask prices (prices offered by sellers). The difference between the buy and sell price is called the bid-ask spread.

The amount that you invest is called the principal or face value. You make investments because you hope to earn a return (your earnings). The rate of return is expressed as a percentage of the principal. Higher rates of return can potentially earn you more money—bringing you even closer to your financial goals.

Own It

A stock is part ownership in a company. Stocks are tracked using their symbols. For example, Apple's stock symbol is AAPL. You can find a company's stock symbol by using a search engine. Stock quotes include:

- Volume (number of stocks bought and sold)
- Ranges for stock prices over time, like a day or fifty-two-week period
- Earnings per share, or a company's profit divided by the number of shares outstanding.
- Price-to-earnings ratio (P/E ratio), or the current market price per share divided by the annual earnings per share

Stocks (and other securities) are traded on stock markets, which serve as both primary and secondary exchanges. A primary exchange allows companies and the government to obtain funding from investors, like you. The secondary market lets investors sell their securities to other investors. There are different stock exchanges throughout the world. For example, the New York Stock Exchange (NYSE) is an actual place with a trading floor, while NASDAQ is a virtual over-the-counter market.

Lend It

A bond is an investment that matches lenders (like you) with borrowers (like companies and governments). When you buy a bond, you are lending your money to a borrower, who is legally obligated to repay your principal with interest. Bond ratings are letters given to bonds that show the likelihood of repayment. The letters are like school grades and range from AAA to D. A government bond with the AAA rating means that you will most likely receive your original investment with interest. But a bond with a D rating means that you will probably lose your investment money!

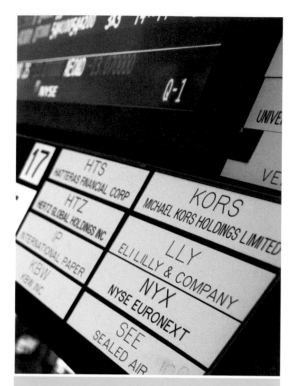

This photograph shows a post on the floor of the NYSE, which displays some of the exchange's stock symbols, including the NYSE Euronext (NYX), an organization that owns several stock markets in the United States and Europe. NYX accounts for one-third of equities (or ownership in investment securities) trading worldwide.

Bond investors know bond terms:

- A bond's face value is called par. A $10,000 Treasury bond has a par of $10,000.
- When bonds "rally," it means their prices increase.
- The coupon refers to the expected interest rate, or amount that you will earn expressed as a percentage.
- Maturity refers to the date when an investor receives the face value of the bond. If an investor holds a bond to maturity, the yield will equal the coupon rate. Sometimes bondholders sell their bonds before the maturity date.
- A bond market is where bonds are bought and sold.
- Brokers are people who trade securities, like stocks and bonds, for a fee called a brokerage commission.

You can hold a short-term bond for one to five years, a medium-term bond for five to twelve years, or a long-term bond for more than twelve years.

Fascinating Financial Fact

'Ihe New York Stock Exchange (NYSE) is the largest stock exchange in the United States. More than 2,500 companies are found on the NYSE.

Outside the Box

Investments include stock and bonds. They also include mutual funds and retirement funds. A 401(k) is a retirement plan where employers contribute pretaxed amounts into specific investments. Money is taxed only when withdrawn. There are also IRAs and Roth IRAs, which allowed for up to $5,000 in 2012 annual contributions for people under the age of fifty. People who were fifty or older could contribute $6,000 that year.

Many investment options earn you money by paying interest. Simple interest is calculated by multiplying principal, interest rate, and time period. To see simple interest in action, think back to Jim's $100 investment. At the end of one year, Jim earned $10 in interest, or $100 (principal) x .10 (interest rate) x 1 (time period in years). Compound interest is what happens when you earn interest on your investment, plus interest on your interest. Suppose Jim's $100 investment was compounded monthly. He would earn $10 in interest on his principal, plus about 50 cents in interest on his interest!

Do you know how long it takes to double your investment money? Use the Rule of 72 to find out. Divide the interest

What the credit rating agencies do

The task of rating agencies is to guide investors about risk levels when buying bonds. All three agencies are accredited by the U.S. Securities and Exchange Commission. They attach one of a series of creditworthiness ratings to governments, municipalities and large corporations. In August, Standard & Poor's downgraded the U.S. debt for the first time in history and a second downgrade, either from Moody's or Fitch, could follow if Congress fails to agree on a credible long-term plan to cut the U.S. deficit. A look at their business:

STANDARD & POOR'S	MOODY'S	Fitch Ratings
• **S&P is known** for its financial research as well as its stock indices in the United States, Australia, Canada, India and Italy	• **Moody's** is the holding company for Moody's Analytics; performs global financial research on countries and firms	• **Fitch** tends to be the agency to which investors turn when the other two of the "Big Three" agencies disagree
• **Market share** about 40 percent	• **Market share** about 40 percent	• **Market share** about 15 percent
• **Headquarters** New York City	• **Headquarters** New York City	• **Headquarters** Paris

Comparing the Big Three's ratings systems

Investment grade		**Investment grade**		**Investment grade**	
Highest quality borrower	AAA	Highest quality	Aaa	Best quality	AAA
High quality borrower	AA	High quality	Aa	Quality companies	AA
Quality borrower	A	Upper-medium	A	Economy can affect finances	A
Medium, satisfactory	BBB	Moderate credit risk	Baa	Medium class companies	BBB
'Junk'		**Speculative, or 'junk'**		**Non-investment grade**	
Prone to economic changes	BB	Questionable credit quality	Ba	Prone to economic changes	BB
Situation varies noticeably	B	Speculative, high credit risk	B	Situation varies noticeably	B
Currently vulnerable	CCC	Low grade, default possible	Caa	Currently vulnerable	CCC
Highly vulnerable, speculative	CC	Highly speculative, usually in partial default	Ca	Highly vulnerable, but still meeting obligations	C
Highly vulnerable, in arrears	C	Low grade, usually in default	C	Partially defaulted, high risk	D
Past due on interest	CI			Not publicly rated	NR

How the U.S. ranks

▶ **S&P's AA+ (high)** ———— ▶ **Moody's Aaa (highest)** ———— ▶ **Fitch AAA (best)**

Source: McClatchy Washington Bureau, Yahoo! Finance, T. Rowe Price, U.S. Department of Treasury, Reuters
Graphic: Robert Dorrell

© 2011 MCT

According to credit agencies, investment grade bonds receive the highest ratings (lowest risk), whereas junk bonds are riskier.

rate into 72. The answer is the number of years it will take to double your money. For example, suppose you make an investment that has a rate of return of 10 percent. According to the Rule of 72, it will take 7.2 years for your money to double—or 72 divided by 10. Now it's your turn. Use the Rule of 72 to find out how long it will take to double your money with 5 percent, 10 percent, and 15 percent rates of return. Did you notice that your money grows fastest with the highest rate of return?

Secret #5

Understand Investment Options

You know about CDs in the music world. But what about CDs in the investment world? How does investing in a government bond help pay for roads? What does it mean to investors when a stock's price increases? CDs, bonds, and stocks are some of your investment options. Successful investors begin by understanding their options. Then they put them together in their portfolios, or collection of securities.

Earning Interest

Certificates of deposit (or CDs) are a kind of investment tool. When you invest in a certificate of deposit, you agree to keep your money in the bank for a certain amount of time (from weeks to years). In return, you usually earn a fixed amount of interest. The interest rate represents your rate of return, or the gain or loss that you expect to receive from an initial investment.

A bond is another investment that can offer fixed interest rates. You buy a bond at face value

Fascinating Financial Fact

A bull market means that investment prices are rising or expected to rise, while a bear market refers to falling investment prices. From 2002 to 2007, it was a bull market in the United States. But 2008 was a bear market, with June being called the "worst month for stocks since the Great Depression" (CNNMoney.com).

(its price) and receive interest (your earnings) until the bond matures. There are intermediate bonds, which mature in three to five years and short-term ones that mature even sooner. Other bonds are long-term, such as the thirty-year Treasury bonds. Bonds are low-risk investments because you will most likely receive the earnings that you expect.

Stock Payoffs

Stocks are on the opposite end of the risk spectrum. A large company, such as Apple (part of the large cap stocks) issues millions of shares, whereas smaller companies issue hundreds or fewer of mid-cap, small-cap, or micro-cap stocks. Investors can earn money from stock dividends, which are parts of a company's profits given in cash. They can also earn money by selling their stocks. Stocks are risky investments because money is easily gained or lost from these sales.

For example, suppose you bought ten stocks for $5 each. Then the stocks' price rises to $7. Did you automatically earn a profit? No, you only earn money when you sell your stock. After the sale, you would make $20. The difference between the purchase price ($5) and the selling price ($7) is called the capital gain. Now imagine that your $5 shares drop to $2 shares. If you sold all of your stocks, you would lose $30 (capital loss). According to CNNMoney.com, investors earn more money from stocks than bonds in the long run. In general, stocks are riskier, but they also yield greater returns.

Put It Together

Mutual funds allow you to invest in several securities together. A mutual fund pools investors' money and then allocates it into different investments. You can choose stock mutual funds or bond mutual funds. You can also invest in asset allocation funds or balanced funds, which include stocks, bonds, and cash.

Stock mutual funds consist of growth, value, and blend funds. Growth funds usually include big companies that have fast sales and earnings growth, such as Wal-Mart. Value funds look for deals, such as companies that have financial problems but are expected to do better in the future. Blend funds combine growth and value funds. For example, a blend fund that follows the Standard & Poor's 500 Index contains both big, steady companies and those with potential growth.

According to the *Investing Bible* by Lynn O'Shaughnessy, the average value fund was less volatile than the average growth fund in the past twenty years. Many mutual funds require minimum initial investments. But these amounts may be avoided if your parent or guardian opens an account for your education or retirement. You must be eighteen or older to invest in stocks, bonds, or mutual funds, unless opening an account with a cosigner such as a parent or legal guardian.

MYTHS
AND
FACTS

Myth

All investments carry the same risk and earn the same returns.

FACT

Different investments have different risks and different returns. Securities with higher risks generally yield higher returns.

Myth

Successful investing includes putting all of your money in one kind of security.

FACT

Successful investing includes diversification, or having different kinds of securities in your investment portfolio. Spread the risk around!

Myth

With investing, it's the short run that counts.

FACT

Focus on long-term average returns and start investing early.

Diversify Your Investments

Diversification is about NOT putting all your eggs in one basket. Successful investing mixes things up, like the mutual funds that include both stocks and bonds. By investing in a variety of options, you can reap the benefits of different rates of return. You can also minimize your investment risk.

The Diversification Difference

Consider two different investment options. Portfolio #1 puts all of your money into the stock market. Portfolio #2 divides your investment money between stocks and bonds. Suppose the economy is growing slowly, and companies are earning less money. Soon stock prices decrease. You lose most (if not all) of the value of your stock investments.

But the bond market continues to yield profits. With Portfolio #1, the value of your entire investment fell. But with Portfolio #2, only part of your investment (the stocks) lost value, while the rest (the bonds) earned money. Diversifying your investments protects you by spreading your financial risk among different investment options.

Think Global

You can diversify within one security (such as investing in many stocks) or between different securities (such as buying both stocks and bonds). You can also diversify by investing in both U.S. and foreign securities. Does this investment combination eliminate risk? No. Risk is part of investing. The global financial world is connected. So economic happenings in one country can affect other countries, too. In other words, bull and bear markets can spread!

For example, suppose you were an investor in the U.S. bull market of 2007. You bought a stock mutual fund that invests in U.S. companies and another one in foreign companies. By 2008, a worldwide economic recession hit. Stock prices in different countries fell drastically, and investors around the world lost billions of dollars. It was one of the worst economic downturns in history. Nothing can protect investors from all risks. But diversification limits risk.

Your Turn to Diversify

Now it's your turn to gain hands-on experience with stocks and bonds—without gaining or losing any real money! Pick five to ten stocks and track their performance. To find stocks, Charles Schwab (a financial services company) encourages teens to 1) consider the stores where they shop; 2) think about the types of goods or services that they consume, like clothing and cell phone contracts; and 3) look around for the businesses in their community.

Once you have chosen your stocks, look in the paper or online to record:

➤ The date
➤ Stock name
➤ Stock symbol
➤ Stock price
➤ Number of stocks bought
➤ Value of your stock investment over time, such as one month

Personal Portfolio Summary

Securities
Money Market Funds and Cash
Certificates
Annuities
Mutual Funds

If you are tracking a stock over a week, you will most likely see small changes in stock prices. Investors evaluate stock prices over the long run to assess average returns.

Date	Stock Name	Stock Symbol	Stock Price	Number of Stocks Bought	Value of Your Stock Investment
10/05/12	Cell Phone 4 U	C4U	$45	2	$90
10/06/12	Cell Phone 4 U	C4U	$44	2	$88
10/07/12	Cell Phone 4 U	C4U	$42	2	$84
10/08/12	Cell Phone 4 U	C4U	$46	2	$92

After tracking your stocks, look at your results. Did the stock prices change a lot? Did the value of your investments increase or decrease? What was the relationship between changes in stock prices and changes in investment values? Now think about the bond market. When you buy a bond, you may receive a fairly steady return—the interest rate—along with your principal when the bond matures.

Finally, think about how these stock and bond returns relate to volatility. Volatility refers to the amount of risk arising from not knowing how much an investment's value will change. Stock returns are much more volatile because there is a greater uncertainty about their actual returns. In general, stocks are riskier investments than bonds. Stocks also yield greater average returns than bonds over the long run.

Back to the Crisis

Let's return to the economic crisis that began in 2007. By 2008, many investors took their money out of the stock

Fascinating Financial Fact

Charles Schwab suggests index mutual funds for teen investors because they have diversification and low costs. An index fund consists of all stocks in a specific index, such as the S&P 500 Index.

market and bought bonds. In some cases, increased demand for bonds drove down their returns to almost zero. But the financial market was such a disaster that investors wanted to receive their principals (original investments)—even if they did not earn extra money. In other words, they just wanted safe havens for their money!

Now think about investors that put their money into single sector funds. These funds lack diversification, so they carry tremendous risk. Bear markets often decrease stock prices in specific industries, such as technology and natural resources. Suppose you owned a single technology sector fund in a bear market, like in 2008. The value of your investment would have plummeted! Of course, investors weigh this risk against the possibility of earning a lot of money from owning a single sector fund in a bull market. Remember that risk and rate of returns often move in opposite directions.

10 GREAT QUESTIONS
to Ask a Financial Adviser

1 How should I allocate stocks, bonds, and cash in my investment portfolio?

2 What kinds of mutual funds are the best investments for young adults?

3 How can I use my budget information to ensure regular investment contributions?

4 What are some investment options for saving for college?

5 Do all investment tools require a parent or guardian to cosign with me?

6 Should I think about retirement now?

7 Do the returns from stocks and bonds usually move in the same direction?

8 Which investments carry the most risk and the least risk?

9 Where can I find out about investment scams?

10 How does economic performance affect my investments?

Play Games

Successful investing is about playing games and joining clubs. You've probably heard the expression "practice makes perfect." Investing is no exception. It takes research, time, money, and practice. Luckily, there are many investing clubs and online investment games that give you hands-on experience. Let's play!

Gen i Revolution

Join the Gen i Revolution from the Council for Economic Education. There are different missions that teach you about investment concepts. Mission 1 reinforces the importance of saving for retirement from a young age—like now! Remember that teens have more time for their investments to grow. In this lesson, join Angela and take the 401(k) Challenge to "build wealth over the long-term." Mission 6 explores the relationship between risk and the rate of return. Help Kai Chung invest his grandmother's gift money so that he can pay for college.

Fascinating Financial Fact

In 2012, Junior Achievement programs were offered in thousands of classrooms in the United States and Canada and had reached more that four million students in each country. Gain work, financial literacy, and business skills by joining today!

Missions 8 through 10 explore the world of stocks, bonds, and mutual funds. In Mission 8, learn how to read a stock table to help Uncle Louie create the best investment portfolio for his nephew. Mission 9 challenges you to help twins Tyrone and Felicia save for college by investing in bonds. Learn about bond ratings and tables. Then simulate an online investment club and explore mutual funds, fund tables, and diversification.

Tracking your stocks, playing an investment game, and financially advising others takes knowledge. Missions 11 through 13 provide this information with tools for company research, stock market basics, and strategies for weathering stock market crashes in bear markets. Click on http://www.genirevolution.org/faqs.php for instructions on how to sign up, play, and complete all these missions.

Sports, Clubs, and Contests

Do you like sports? Then, Visa has online games for you! Its Financial Football and Financial Soccer test your knowledge

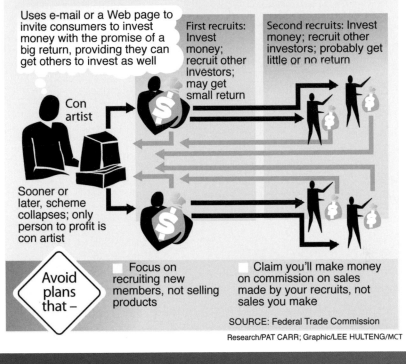

Investors beware

The Federal Trade Commission is cracking down on so-called pyramid schemes on the Internet. How a typical scheme works:

Uses e-mail or a Web page to invite consumers to invest money with the promise of a big return, providing they can get others to invest as well

Con artist

First recruits: Invest money; recruit other investors; may get small return

Second recruits: Invest money; recruit other investors; probably get little or no return

Sooner or later, scheme collapses; only person to profit is con artist

Avoid plans that –

Focus on recruiting new members, not selling products

Claim you'll make money on commission on sales made by your recruits, not sales you make

SOURCE: Federal Trade Commission

Research/PAT CARR; Graphic/LEE HULTENG/MCT

A pyramid scheme is an investment scam. Read the Federal Trade Commission's warnings to avoid losing your money.

of financial concepts, like investment tools. Financially empower yourself while scoring touchdowns and goals, and winning games. Visit http://www.practicalmoneyskills.com /games/trainingcamp to join the football team or http:// www.financialsoccer.com to play soccer.

Many schools and communities offer investment clubs. Find out if your school has a club that allows you to gain real-life investment experience. If not, approach a teacher about starting one. Investment clubs help teens acquire knowledge, gain experience, and earn money. They also connect teens with mentors and peers with investment interests. Learning investment strategies today will better prepare you for financial success tomorrow.

You can also research investment contests online and enter with your club or school. For example, the CNBC Student Stock Tournament once offered students in grades 4–12 the opportunity to compete for weekly $1,000 prizes, 200 shares of GE stocks worth about $20,000, and a $5,000 school endowment. Colleges and companies also provide opportunities for investment contests, with prizes that include thousands of dollars.

Don't Be Scammed

Finally, beware of investment scams! There are many "get rich quick" schemes and cases of Internet fraud. According to USA.gov, look for warning signs, including salespeople that 1) encourage you to borrow money for investing; 2) pressure you to act now; 3) promise big returns quickly; and 4) use words like "guarantee," "limited offer," and "high return." If you are considering hiring a potential broker or brokerage firm that invests on your behalf, do the research at the Financial Industry Regulatory Authority's Central Registration Depository site.

Also, find out if your school offers the North American Securities Administrators Association's (NASAA) free Fraud Scene Investigator (FSI) program. In the first FSI assignment, "Suitable Investments," learn how to fight fraud and capture "Mr. X" by analyzing stock tables, examining companies online, and uncovering sales scams. The NASAA's podcasts also offer advice on being an alert investor. Check them out at http://www.nasaa.org/newsroom/nasaa-podcast-archive.

Think About Retirement Now

Successful investing means thinking ahead. You will probably work, spend, save, and invest for decades until you retire. Most people retire, or stop working for good, around the age of sixty-five. Retired people no longer receive job income, but they still have bills to pay. Most receive certain monetary government benefits, like Social Security. But these benefits alone will probably not pay for their current lifestyles. The money to pay for many of their expenses comes from their investments.

Remember the two things that will most likely increase your investments: more money and time. Retirement investments involve both! As a teen, you have about fifty years before you stop working. But you will also need a lot of money by then to afford your lifestyle. Inflation, or a rise in the prices of commonly used goods and services, will only make things more costly. To prepare for retirement, people save and invest throughout their working years. Many successful investors begin even earlier—like now!

Fascinating Financial Fact

According to a U.S. Government Accountability Office report, an "estimated 36.8 percent of today's seventeen-year-olds will have no money in a 401(k) or similar plan when they retire. The numbers will be worse for low-income workers: 63 percent of them will have zero dollars in a 401(k)-type account when it comes time for them to retire."

401(k) Plan

One of the most popular retirement funds is the 401(k) plan. According to the *Investing Bible* by Lynn O'Shaughnessy, eight out of ten people "have already enrolled in a 401(k)." O'Shaughnessy also says that you would have $1.1 million if you saved $400 each month for 30 years in a 401(k) plan that yields 11 percent. A 401(k) plan is an investment portfolio of your choice, which can consist of domestic and/or international stocks, bonds, and cash.

A 401(k) plan begins when your employer takes regular contributions out of your paycheck and invests them in your chosen portfolio. Employers can match your deposits and usually contribute 50 cents for every $1 that you invest until they reach 6 percent of your salary. For example, suppose that you earn $60,000 each year. You decide to invest 6 percent, or $3,600 into a 401(k) plan. Your employer contributes 50 percent, or $1,800 to your plan, too. As a result, you now have an annual contribution of $5,400 to your 401(k) plan.

Generate more money for your future by saving for retirement now. If you have taxable income, you could ask your parents to help you set up a Roth IRA online. Perhaps your parents will match your IRA contributions.

401(k) plans have other advantages, like tax benefits and high ceilings. Taxes are government fees that people pay on things, such as income and profits. Although many investments require you to pay taxes, deposits and earnings from a 401(k) plan are tax-free. However, you are taxed at your income tax rate when you withdraw your money. The maximum annual contribution allowed for a 401(k) plan was $17,500 in 2013.

And don't worry about your 401(k) plan if you change jobs! You have options, like putting all or some of your money into an IRA rollover, letting the money stay with your former company's plan, or placing your money into a new 401(k). Whatever you do, try to keep your money in a retirement fund. Many young people cash their funds in and spend them. But successful investors reap the benefits of long-term gains.

Individual Retirement Accounts (IRAs)

IRAs are federally sponsored individual retirement plans. In 2013, you could invest up to $5,500 in an IRA with a financial institution, such as a bank or mutual fund firm. Maximum contributions may change each year. Visit the Internal Revenue Service (IRS) site for the latest information and explore your IRA options:

- Deductible IRAs offer tax-deferred earnings.
- Nondeductible IRAs require paying taxes on deposits and withdrawals.
- Roth IRAs may offer tax-free deposits, earnings, and withdrawals.

The first thing that you need for a Roth IRA is taxable income. If you work after school, on weekends, or in the summer, you meet the requirement. Ask your parent or guardian to set up the Roth IRA for you. The process can be done quickly online and requires your Social Security number, employer name and address, bank information, and money amount for transfer to the IRA. Challenge your parents to match your contributions!

Don't Forget About Taxes

Successful investing means understanding taxes. You already know that taxes are government fees charged on income, various goods and services, and some investment yields. The investment money that you can eventually spend partly depends on the government's share. Like retirement plans, stock and bond investments have different tax rules. The key is to know your investment's after-tax return.

Benjamin Franklin once said, "The only things certain in life are death and taxes." Taxes may be certain, but it pays to look at some strategies for how to minimize them. Can timing affect the amount of taxes that you pay? Are there tax-free bonds? Do tax-exempt mutual funds exist? Choosing certain investments can lower your tax burden and keep more gains in your pocket.

Taxing Profits

Investors pay short-term capital gains taxes when they sell their investments after holding them for less than one year. For example, suppose you invested in a stock mutual fund. After six months, you closed the account and withdrew your deposit plus your earnings. You would pay a short-term capital gains tax on your earnings. These profits are taxed at the same rate as your income. How can you avoid paying short-term taxes? Hold your investments for more than one year!

Long-term capital gains taxes are paid on investment profits that are sold after owning them for more than one year. These taxes are paid more frequently on stock investments than bond ones. Most bond investors pay taxes on

Accountants and financial planners can answer your individual tax and investment questions.

the interest earned from their investments. Bondholders can choose to reinvest this income, or put it back into an investment. They can also choose to keep the interest money for spending. Either way, bondholders pay taxes on their interest income at a rate equal to their income brackets with a ceiling of 15 percent.

As a stock investor, you may pay dividend taxes on your investments. Remember that a dividend is the part of a company's earnings paid out to investors. These earnings are distributed per share. If you owned fifty shares, you would receive more dividends than an investor with only twenty shares. Investors can choose to pocket the money or reinvest their dividends. In both cases, the government taxes these dividends at the same rate as your income.

Bond Income Tax Strategies

Bond investors pay taxes on interest earned from different bond investments. State, local, and federal governments issue bonds to borrow money and pay for expenses,

Fascinating Financial Fact

A house is a type of capital asset. According to the Internal Revenue Service, you must report capital gains received when you sell your house at a profit. However, you cannot deduct capital losses on property used for personal reasons (like living in it!).

such as building roads. State and local governments offer municipal bonds. You do not have to pay federal taxes on municipal bonds. This keeps more of the earnings in your pocket. Municipal bonds, also known as tax-free or tax-exempt bonds, give tax protection. But they also tend to offer lower interest rates than other bonds. Another trade-off!

More bond strategies include researching tax-free bond options offered by investment companies. Compare the interest rates of different bonds. Remember that higher interest rates yield higher returns. Many analysts also do not recommend putting tax-free bonds into a retirement account because these accounts are already tax-protected. Finally, maximize your bond earnings by jumping ship when needed. If you own a bond that is losing its value, swap it. Sell the bond, claim the lost money as a tax deduction, and buy a more valuable investment.

More Tax-Free Options

Explore mutual funds that offer tax protection because they contain tax-free bonds. Do the research and find mutual funds that allow you to keep more of your earnings. For example, look at Kiplinger.com's ratings for long-term municipal bonds. Did you find investments that offer relatively high yields and tax protection? If so, remember that you can still opt for investments with higher taxable returns. Making an investment is a personal choice.

Would you like to receive tax protection and pay for college? Explore the Education IRA (also known as the Coverdell ESA). The Education IRA is used to pay for future education expenses from nursery school through college. In 2012, a parent or guardian could make an annual contribution of up to $2,000. Contributions are allowed until a child reaches the age of eighteen. Special needs children may receive contributions to an Education IRA for longer periods of time. All of these savings are tax-free—including at the time of withdrawal, if the money is used for education.

Each state also offers another tax-free way to pay for education—the 529 Plan. This plan is specifically for college expenses. Deposits in a 529 plan grow tax-free. When withdrawn, money is subject to taxes—but at the student's lower tax bracket rate. There are also some states, such as New York, Wisconsin, Michigan, and Oregon, that allow investors to receive state tax deductions on their contributions. To find out about the 529 in your state, visit the College Savings Plan Network at www.collegesavings.org.

Stay Informed

Successful investing means being aware of the changes in the economy and its financial markets. These changes affect the values of your investments. Being informed allows investors to choose the best investment tools, given the available information. As shown by the 2007–2009 global recession, no one, including investors, can predict the future. But there are indicators that can guide you in making and tracking your investment decisions.

Stock Market Indexes

You cannot follow every stock in your portfolio. But you can gauge trends in the stock market by following stock indexes. These indexes represent stock market prices:

> ➤ Standard and Poor's 500 Index (S&P 500) is a group of 500 large cap stocks that represents the risks and returns of the U.S. equity markets. The top three

A stockbroker makes investment decisions for individuals and companies by keeping informed about market changes, including Federal Reserve announcements about interest rates.

industries in the S&P 500 are information technology (like Microsoft), financials (such as Bank of America), and energy (think Chevron).

➤ Dow Jones Industrial Average (DJIA) represents only thirty of America's largest corporations. Large market capitalization (or large cap) companies have more than $10 billion in the market value of their outstanding shares.

Do you remember the U.S. financial crisis that began in 2007? Take a look at the indexes to find out what happened to the stock prices of major U.S. companies. By

Fascinating Financial Fact

During the 2007–2009 recession, the Federal Reserve decreased the federal funds interest rate to its lowest level in history.

September 2008, the DJIA suffered its biggest drop in history, falling 778 points. At that time, the value of the stocks in the S&P Index companies decreased by more than $600 billion. These indexes serve as indicators of economic performance. In the case of the financial crisis, the stock market was one sign of the coming worldwide recession, or slowdown in economic growth.

By following a stock market index online, you can find out valuable information about the direction of the stock market. Does the trend indicate a bear or bull market? How volatile are the S&P Index and Dow Jones Industrial Average? Chances are that you will invest in large cap companies either directly or in a mutual fund. Start tracking them now by visiting sites, like http://money.cnn.com/data/markets/sandp. Many large cap mutual funds are aligned to the S&P Index, so this index is a good indicator of how these mutual funds perform.

Interested in the Federal Reserve

You already know that the interest rate is the return on a bond. Different bonds offer different interest rates. The interest rate on U.S. Treasuries (or debt secured by the federal government) is an important determinant of other bond rates. Bonds that are riskier than U.S. Treasuries offer higher interest rates. This is another example of the risk-rate of return trade-off!

The Federal Reserve (U.S. central bank) determines a short-term interest rate that influences bond returns. It conducts monetary policy, which involves manipulating the interest rates to affect economic performance. Think about how interest rates affect consumption and investments. People and businesses borrow money to spend and invest.

Some high schools offer investment clubs that allow teens to track the stock market. Student members meet with faculty advisers a couple of times each month to discuss stock market information, companies, investment trends, and so forth, and then vote on their investment strategy. Decisions are determined by majority rule.

When they take out loans, they pay interest. So interest is also the cost of borrowing money.

> ➤ If interest rates are low, then more people and businesses will borrow, spend, and invest money.
> ➤ If interest rates are high, then fewer people will borrow, spend, and invest money.

By influencing the cost of borrowing money, the Federal Reserve can affect consumption (individual purchases of goods and services) and investment. Consumption and investment mainly determine how much an economy grows. When consumption and investment increase, the economy is growing. But fewer expenditures by individuals and businesses mean less economic growth.

Keep track of the Federal Reserve's monetary policy to determine expected interest rates for bonds. The Federal Reserve often uses this policy to control inflation, or a rise in the prices of commonly used goods and services. When the economy is growing, it puts pressure on prices to rise. So the Federal Reserve will often increase interest rates to slow economic growth and rising prices. On the flip side, when the economy is shrinking, or growing slowly, the Federal Reserve often lowers interest rates to spur economic growth.

Look for Signs

Signs of economic growth or rising prices include:

- Increase in gross domestic product, GDP (or dollar amount of total output in a country)

- Increase in consumer price index (which measures changes in price level)
- Decrease in the unemployment rate (or the number of people out of work, but actively looking)
- Increase in building construction

In all these cases, the Federal Reserve will often increase interest rates to discourage consumption and investment and slow economic growth and rising prices. When interest rates rise, bond prices fall because their rates of return increase. On the flip side, the Federal Reserve lowers interest rates to increase consumption, investment, and economic growth during economic downturns. Falling interest rates decrease bond yields and increase bond prices.

Remember that you want to earn high returns over the long run from your investments so that you can afford your future financial goals. Invest successfully by understanding your inner investor, speaking the financial language, knowing your options, doing the research, and staying informed.

Glossary

bear market A period of expected or actual falling investment prices.

bond Investment in which a person loans money to a borrower for a certain amount of time at a specific interest rate.

bull market A period of expected or actual rising investment prices.

diversification Inclusion of different kinds of investments in one portfolio.

401(k) plan An employer plan in which employees contribute part of their salaries on a post-tax and/or pre-tax basis.

individual retirement account (IRA) Investment retirement fund.

interest The cost of borrowing money or return on an investment.

investment A good or asset that is purchased in hopes of earning money.

mutual fund Security that pools together investors' money and then allocates it into different investments.

rate of return Earnings expressed as a percentage of the principal.

risk The chance that things will turn out differently than expected.

savings Disposable income minus expenses.

security A type of investment, like stocks or bonds.

stock Ownership in a company with a claim on part of the company's assets and earnings.

For More Information

Bank of Canada
Public Information
234 Wellington Street
Ottawa, ON K1A 0G9
Canada
(613) 782-8111
Web site: http://www.bank-banque-canada.ca
The Bank of Canada is Canada's central bank. Its monetary
  policy affects interest rates.

Board of Governors of the Federal Reserve System
20th Street and Constitution Avenue NW
Washington, DC 20551
Web site: http://www.federalreserve.gov
The Federal Reserve is the United States' central bank. Its
  monetary policy influences interest rates.

Council for Economic Education
122 East 42nd Street, Suite 2600
New York, NY 10168
(800) 338-1192
Web site: http://www.councilforeconed.org
The Council for Economic Education is the leading U.S.
  organization for economics and financial education.

Junior Achievement (JA)
Canada Headquarters
1 Eva Road, Suite 218
Toronto, ON M9C 4Z5
Canada
(416) 622-4602
Web site: http://jacan.org
With programs across Canada, Junior Achievement pro-
motes entrepreneurship, financial literacy, and work
readiness among students.

Junior Achievement (JA)
USA Headquarters
One Education Way
Colorado Springs, CO 80906
(719) 540-8000
Web site: http://www.ja.org
With programs throughout the United States, Junior
Achievement is a nonprofit organization that helps stu-
dents gain the knowledge and skills for financial success.

Web Sites

Due to the changing nature of Internet links, Rosen Publishing
has developed an online list of Web sites related to the subject of this book. This site is updated regularly. Please use
this link to access the list:

http://www.rosenlinks.com/SGFE/Invst

For Further Reading

Batcman, Katherine R. *The Young Investor: Projects and Activities for Making Your Money Grow.* Chicago, IL: Chicago Review Press, 2010.

Constable, Simon, and Robert E. Wright. *The WSJ Guide to the 50 Economic Indicators That Really Matter: From Big Macs to "Zombie Banks," the Indicators Smart Investors Watch to Beat the Market.* New York, NY: HarperCollins, 2011.

Gardner, David, Tom Gardner, and Selena Maranjian. *The Motley Fool Investment Guide for Teens: 8 Steps to Having More Money Than Your Parents Ever Dreamed Of.* New York, NY: Fireside, 2002.

Hall, Alvin D. *Getting Started in Mutual Funds.* Hoboken, NJ: Wiley Publishing, Inc., 2010.

Hurley, Joseph F. *The Best Way to Save for College: A Complete Guide to 529 Plans 2011–12.* Pittsford, NY: JFH Innovative LLC, 2011.

Karlitz, Gail. *Growing Money: A Complete Investing Guide for Kids.* New York, NY: Price Stern Sloan, 2010.

MarksJarvis, Gail. *Saving for Retirement (Without Living Like a Pauper or Winning the Lottery).* Upper Saddle River, NJ: FT Press, 2012.

Mladjenovic, Paul. *Stock Investing for Dummies.* Hoboken, NJ: Wiley Publishing, Inc., 2009.

Wild, Russell. *Bond Investing for Dummies.* Hoboken, NJ: Wiley Publishing, Inc., 2007.

Bibliography

Charles Schwab. "Ready, Set, Invest! How to Get Your Teen
    Started in Investing." Mutual Fund Education Alliance,
    2006. Retrieved October 2012 (http://www.mfea.com
    /investmentgoals/investingchildren/investingforkids
    /SchwabTeensInvest.pdf).

Forbes. "Average Price of a New Car?" May 10, 2012.
    Retrieved October 2012 (http://www.forbes.com/sites
    /moneybuilder/2012/05/10/average-price-of-a-new-car).

Gandel, Stephen. "Bear Market Guide: Relax, Make Money."
    CNN Money, June 29, 2008. Retrieved October 2012
    (http://money.cnn.com/2008/06/27/markets/bear
    _market.moneymag/index.htm).

Institute of Education Sciences. "Fast Facts: Tuition Costs of
    College and Universities." National Center for Education
    Statistics. Retrieved October 2012 (http://nces.ed.gov
    /fastfacts/display.asp?id=76).

IRS. "401(k) Resource Guide - Plan Participants - Limitation
    on Elective Deferrals." Retrieved October 2012 (http://
    www.irs.gov/Retirement-Plans/Plan-Participant,
    -Employee/401(k)-Resource-Guide---Plan-Participants
    ---Limitation-on-Elective-Deferrals).

Junior Achievement. "About JA." Retrieved October 2012
    (http://www.ja.org/about/about.shtml).

Kadlec, Dan. "Kids and Money: Start Them Early with a
    Family 401(k)." CBS Moneywatch, November 22, 2010.

Retrieved October 2012 (http://www.cbsnews.com
/8301-505146_162-42140461/kids-and-money
-start-them-early-with-a-family-401k).

North American Securities Administrators Association. "The
FYI on FSI." Retrieved October 2012 (http://www.nasaa
.org/wp-content/uploads/2011/08/FYI-on-FSI.pdf).

O'Shaughnessy, Lynn. *Investing Bible*. Hoboken, NJ: Wiley
Publishing, Inc., 2001.

PR Newswire. "The CNBC Student Stock Tournament
Presented by Lincoln Financial Group Kicks-Off the
1999 Fall Semester." 2012. Retrieved October 2012
(http://www.prnewswire.com/news-releases/the-cnbc
-student-stock-tournament-presented-by-lincoln
-financial-group-kicks-off-the-1999-fall-semester
-74465727.html).

USA.gov. "Beware of Investment Fraud." October 17, 2012.
Retrieved October 2012 (http://www.usa.gov/topics
/consumer/scams-fraud/investment.shtml).

Vohwinkle, Jeremy. "Teens Don't Save for Retirement."
Retrieved October 2012 (http://genxfinance.com
/teens-dont-save-for-retirement-are-you-surprised).

Wells Fargo. "Investing Basics Minimize Investment Taxes."
Retrieved October 2012 (https://www.wellsfargo.com
/investing/basics/minimize_taxes).

YCharts. "U.S. Average Sales Price for New Houses Sold:
292,400 USD for Sep 2012." November 12, 2012
(http://ycharts.com/indicators/average_sales_price_for
_new_houses_sold_in_the_us).

Index

About the Author

Barbara Gottfried Hollander has authored several economics and business books, including *Top 10 Secrets for Spending Your Money Wisely*; *Money Matters: An Introduction to Economics*; *Managing Money*; *Paying for College: Practical, Creative Strategies*; and *How Credit Crises Happen*. She is an economics and personal finance content developer for online educational companies and an author with the Council for Economic Education. She received a B.A. in economics from the University of Michigan and an M.A. in economics from New York University, specializing in statistics and econometrics and international economics.

Photo Credits

Cover PhotoAlto/Laurence Mouton/Getty Images; back cover, p. 33, multiple interior pages background image iStockphoto/Thinkstock; pp. 4, 24 © AP Images; p. 9 John Lund/Marc Romanelli/Blend Images/Getty Images; p. 10 Rafael Ramirez Lee/Shutterstock.com; p. 13 Laura Gangi Pond/Shutterstock.com; p. 15 Mike Flippo/Shutterstock.com; p. 18 Reggie Casagrande/The Image Bank/Getty Images; p. 26 Dorrell/MCT/Newscom; p. 39 Hulteng KRT/Newscom; p. 43 Dougal Waters/Digital Vision/Getty Images; p. 46 Blend Images/Ariel Skelley/the Agency Collection/Getty Images; p. 51 Mario Tama/Getty Images; p. 53 Goodluz/Shutterstock.com.

Designer: Brian Garvey; Editor: Kathy Kuhtz Campbell; Photo Researcher: Karen Huang